Fire IN THE Heart

GREGORY MULLER

iUniverse, Inc.
New York   Bloomington

Fire in the Heart

iUniverse books may be ordered through booksellers or by contacting:

iUniverse
1663 Liberty Drive
Bloomington, IN 47403
www.iuniverse.com
1-800-Authors (1-800-288-4677)

Because of the dynamic nature of the Internet, any Web addresses or links contained in this book may have changed since publication and may no longer be valid. The views expressed in this work are solely those of the author and do not necessarily reflect the views of the publisher, and the publisher hereby disclaims any responsibility for them.

ISBN: 978-1-4502-4123-6 (pbk)
ISBN: 978-1-4502-4124-3 (ebk)

Printed in the United States of America

iUniverse rev. date: 7/1/10

CONTENTS

Accident 1

Acrobat 2

Acts of Insanity 3

Angelique 4

Apples 5

Arrhythmia 6

Artichoke 7

Beer Bottles 8

Bender... 9

Better or Worse 11

Blanks 12

Blue... 13

Bone 14

Brie 15

Brown 17

Cat's-Eyed Girl 18

Ceiling Tile 20

Celebrate 21

CEO 23

Changes 24

Chirp 25

The Clerk 26

Closed Elevator 27

Cold Bed.. 28

Communion 29

Concert.. 31

Confession 32

Conjunctive Residues 34

Cote D'Azur... 35

Coven 36

Cyberpoems 37

Daydream 38
December and Disability 39
Deception 40
Distribution of Artifacts 41
Don't 43
Dust 44
Dutch Treat 45
Duty 46
Easter 47
Fire in the Heart 48
Fish Eyes 50
Fountainhead 52
Fragment 53
Frogs 54
Fugue 55
The Gardener 58
God 59
God: Then and Now 60
The Grape 61
Grayscale 62
Hiding 63
Hospital Visit 64
I Believe 65
I go away 67
Injustice 68
Interlude 69
Jazz 70
Jesus Beast 71
Laura 73
Light 74
A Lightness of Mind 75
Lima 76
Looking 77
Losing My Religion 78
Lovers' Plans 79

Lust 80
Memories 81
Metamorphosis 82
Michelangelo 83
Mist 84
Moments 85
Moonface 86
Mother Earth 87
The New Millennium 88
New Mood 90
News at Five 91
Nuns 92
Oblivion 93
October 94
Old Men 95
The One-Eyed Prostitute 96
Opening the Gate 97
Pest 98
Pictures 100
The Poet 101
Possibilities 102
Potato Soup 103
A Prayer for Father 105
Primate 106
Prime 108
The Primitive 109
Raspberry Summer 110
Ravena 111
Reason 112
Red Dawn 113
Red Hot Chili Pepper 114
Reservation 115
Rittenhouse Square 116
Road Nap 117
The Rose 118

Sandra 119
Satan 120
Scents 121
Sestina 122
Shadow talk 124
Shimmer 125
Silly Putty 126
Simon 128
Single Scull 129
Skin Deep 130
Slumber 131
Spring Thaw 132
Stardog 133
Stealth Mosquito 135
Stilton 138
Stone Pony 139
The Storm 140
Summer Samba 142
Sunshine 143
Susan 144
Sushi 146
Tea 147
Thanatos 148
Thistles 149
Thunder 150
Transplant 151
Uncle Bob 152
Vegetables 153
Whore 154
Winston 155
Wish 156
Women 157
Words 158

Accident

Blood splattered onto the torn shirt.
In the windswept field,
Beyond the old barn, a tractor
Sat rusting in the weeds.

A dog ran from the shanty and barked.
Two passing trucks swirled-up a cloud of dust;
Jenny ran from the kitchen,
Panting toward the tool shed, with her knife
Flashing in the noonday sun.

The cries got louder;
Now she could see.
His hand was crushed,
Full of splinters, trapped
Under a fallen beam.

Her back to the beam
One push set it free.
Nothing to be salvaged though.
She knew it,
And so did he.

Acrobat

Harlot whore herald angel harlequin
Badger brandy battlements on beams
Of bent board billing boxes.

As Jack's beans bounce in the bone yard wheat field
An airy acrobat stands on steel
Perched at the peak of peril's pond
Stepping, swaying, sweating

Gone is the tarp of justice, stolen
In the darkness of a missing moon.

Balance bends boldly to the brassy blues
Breaking bluntly from the trumpet's core.
His hay stack girl
Abused the tool
But the acrobat
Must pay.

Acts of Insanity

I resolve every day to perform acts of insanity,
To be insane in the morning drive,
To be insane at work,
And to be insane again
On the way home.

Lunch will be a plate of low-fat insanities
Served on a bed of steamed rice.
Exercise periods will be mad
And I will hallucinate while at rest.

Upon waking,
I shall wash in the shower of insanity
With the soap of the unbalanced
And the shampoo of the unstable.

I swear on the Altar of Insanity
To abide by the Code of Insanity
So help me God
Now
And forever
Amen.

Angelique

Angelique de Mozambique
N'a jamais vu de grande boutique
Mais elle connait le rock and roll
Et quelque chose de birth control.

Elle restait toujours a la maison
Pour la plupart des saisons.
Mais elle avait les ideas en tete
Parce qu'elle jouait sur l'Internet.
Elle savait tout! Cette jolie mome!
Sauf les bras d'un gentilhomme.

Angelique de Mozambique
Never saw a large boutique.
But she knew her rock and roll
And something about birth control.

She was one who stayed inside
As the seasons passed her by.
This she did without regret
Because she surfed the Internet.
She knew it all! This cyber fan!
Except the warm arms of a man.

Apples

Father's favorite apple trees
Grow scrawny among the weeds
The old estate is crumbling--
With no one left to care.

I helped him when I was young
Spraying, trimming
Raking up the fallen ones.
He was robust
With a ruddy complexion.

I have seen the apples fall from the tree
Every season
But the year of father's death
They seemed to fall from the tree
Not one by one but simultaneously
All at once.

I have grown old
And the apples
Fall one at a time now
Each time bringing
Up a thought of father.

Arrhythmia

I'm a tired, cold, sick pulse-taker;
They just installed a dual pacemaker.
Next they split my sturdy ribs
To make room for the heart defibs
Fleshy tissue ruins the pace
Makes it slow
Then makes it race
Next come shocks to
Make it right
And send away my appetite.
Lots of pain and lots of worry
Won't be home in such a hurry.

Artichoke

Fleshy, prickly leaves
Pale and limp from heat
Tired sentries
Give way

Tugged
Skinned
Discarded

Raw heart
Vulnerable now
Touched

At last

Beer Bottles

Beer bottles lie shattered in the lane
Meager harvest of a barren winter
The inkwell man forecloses
Winter passes
Cold and bitter

Bender

Twinkle, twinkle little star
Wound up in a crowded bar
How I got here I don't know.
Memories of a theatre show
Of something vulgar something vain
Are streaking through my beer soaked brain.

First a question then a plea
My gang they really wanted me
To go out for a drink or two
And have a laugh to change our view
I checked my wallet for some dough
And down to Rouge we all did go.

First a beer and then a scotch
And then we kicked it up a notch
Beer and scotch and scotch and beer
And soon I found another gear
Finally out the door I went
With a beer and quite a scent

I wandered into Blue next door
Where I drank a little more
Soon my head began to spin
Too much scotch and too much gin
I finally stood up from my stool
And tottered like a drunken fool

Out of the door into the street
The pavement moved beneath my feet
The street lights they were all a blur
My mouth it felt all full of fur
My house was just four blocks away
Four blocks of weave and swerve and sway

It seemed to be my shocking fate
To wake up in the Diamond State
In a bed whose sheets were blue
Without my jacket and one shoe
Sans my clothing sans my dough
In a state of vertigo

Don't tell me. I don't want to know
Just want to find my clothes and go
Bad theatre made me go berserk
And turned me into quite a jerk
Please point me toward the door my friend
And I'll bring this saga to an end.

Better or Worse

It could be better
It could be worse
You could be riding in a hearse
Or waiting for the night shift nurse
Or writing poems in blank blank verse.

You could be all messed up, my friend,
And waiting for your time to end
While stumbling blindly in the dark
As you drink Popov in the park.

But you are here
And now is now
So wipe those blood stains from your brow
And please remove that thorny crown
Before self pity takes you down.

Life has lows
And life has highs
And life is full of compromise.
We endure despite the cost
Only dullness makes us lost.

Blanks

Love fills in the blanks
Blanks
That's right
Blanks
I've got blanks
A lot of blanks
You've got blanks
A lot of blanks
We've all got blanks
More or less
If a blank gets filled
You get less blank
Love fills in the blanks

I can fill up your blanks
If you'd let me.
As far as blanks,
Less is more,
Soon things look different
Than before --
Smooch baby
Smooch

Blue

Blue is the color of the ocean,
The sky, my father's eyes, my jeans,
My paintings, certain flowers of spring,
My fantasies. Blue is the sound of my music.

Blue is the color of my mother's hair
Blue is the color of her hospital gown
Blue are her veins from too many blood transfusions
Blue is the mood of a woman fighting cancer.

Visions of the sky outside her window
Remind her of her own isolation.
While the oscillations of the infusion pump
Deliver chemotherapy through her blue veins
She dozes in her chair
Weak from the ordeal, her lips turn
A light shade of blue.

Bone

Long, tan, dexterous fingers poke
Through the bony pores of the eyes,
One time a space for a vision
Now a worm.
Solid bone
Never to feel pain
Again. Never.
Never mind
Never matter
Never to see atrocities
Peaceful soil-covered
Bone.

Brie

She told me about Jesus and Buddha and Blake
Said coke is OK if you watch what you take
Freud and Jung and Kafka and Pinter
Hexagonal flakes mean a long hard winter

Pillsbury bake-offs
Victorian whores
Black leather jackets
And secret closed doors

Curious cosmos
And didly-dit-dote
Obsequious waiters
That tickled her throat

I reached for a cracker
And then for some cheese
As I scratched at my head
To shake off some fleas

I said
"Is that so"

Oh yes, and there's more
"If you'll open your eyes
I'll sing an encore"

It's called "Whistling in the wind
On an August night,
I'll spread my legs
If it goes just right
Then Genghis Khan comes rushing in
And Jesus Christ says that's a sin,
While the Michelin man plays the violin
And the fat boys and girls
Eat Sugar Twin"

My musical mind was spinning like wild,
My brain was cooking like Julia Child
My lips started to move like I couldn't believe
My speech got all slurry
And my chest gave a heave.

She stood and she looked
With her hands on her hips
Her eyes were a-glowing
She was licking her lips.

I stood and I trembled
And I though for a while
Then I slid on over
And kissed on her smile.

I turned out the lights
And I pressed her to me
Good Lord!
This was better
Than that hard-hearted Brie

Brown

Brown is underrated,
But Brown will bring you around.

I slept on Brown
Ate Brown
Dreamed Brown
And Brown became an obsession.

Its look
Its feel
Its smell
It was good.
I lusted for it.

No ugly green
No hideous blue
Red is the color of death.
But brown is the ultimate sound.

It fills all of your senses;
All cravings come in Brown,
Unbridled Brown.

Not square
Not round
Not anything but Brown.

Brown. Just Brown.

Brown is the consummate textural paste.

Cat's-Eyed Girl

We're near the danger zone.
Kathy paints her face because
She is a whore. Long ago
In a blue wading pool
On a lawn full of weeds
Mother let her sink
To the bottom
So now, a young girl sings for her supper
With twitching legs and rising
Hips.

Her dog ran away and her
Mother saw him go;
She did nothing to help.

His jacket is threadbare.
His eyes set deeply in the sockets.
Mother knew
The blood on his sheets
Was not his own;
She did nothing to help.

In a small kitchen,
Kathy stirs the vegetables in a pot.
Soup for two, but her friend
Does not come.
Never mind.

Happy New Year is waiting;
With lots of work.
The cat's-eyed girl
Stirs that soup and eats.
She knows a fragile whore
Has no use,
Especially
On New Year's Eve.

Ceiling Tile

Waves of feelings pulsatile,
While staring at a ceiling tile,
Wash over me with primal rage,
And spill onto this written page.
Rage is death
And cuts a breath
From every hour
I have left.

It moves my mind
Through the unkind
Memory of a father
Blind. Left alone
And left to wait, left
Because I wept
Too late
For him and for his
Humanity.

Celebrate

There are times when I see far enough
There are times when I can hardly see at all.
Before we leave this planet we must apologize
For our homogeneous state of mind.
Religion through the blender is a bad idea.

I don't puree my meals in the blender
Because they taste like shit.
I don't puree my cheese into a paste
Because that tastes like shit too.
Stilton, Brie, and Camembert
Should stand alone.

Let the dim-witted get drunk
On ecumenical cocktails!
I'll take the single-malt;
That always proves magical for me
And my religious inclinations.
Two fingers. No ice. No mixing.

At graduation I knew that
Beverage experience
Had been the key
To rebuilding
My modern
Spiritual
Life

Now I drink less
And I never mix beverages.
And now I shape myself
With a sculptor's hand

Chipping the stone of my identity
Into a special shape
Among the yes and yes sleeping blockheads
Of these modern times.
I build rough edges. Sharp points.
And a delicious granularity of the soul.

CEO

He told us a red rocket of lies,
And followed-up with a twirling-yellow
Space Station of Deception.

When I,
Johnny Blue Cape,
Showed the lie at the
Technicolor Lunchmeat Drive-In Cinema

He hopped a moonbeam to oblivion
And shoved-off toward a galaxy
Of fractured asteroids
And recycled Stardust.

Changes

Raging lust, skin and sunshine
You with your pink cotton shirt
Me with my painter's pants.

Sleeping and eating and making love
Eating and sleeping and making love
Long beach ball days
Baking in Coppertone.

Me with my urgent needs
You with your books
And crystal earrings, flashing
In the sun.

Where exactly,
Did we change our minds?
Was it at your dormitory
Last fall? Or was it at
My apartment
Last summer?

Now you see me
As I pick-up my morning coffee.
Me with my pressed gray pants
You with your stylish earrings
Sleeping and eating and working hard
Eating and sleeping and working hard
Living the frantic days
Of hot coffee and tea,
Moving together
Our separate ways.

Chirp

Leaving the nest
Weathering the storm
Racing home to find
A dead parent.

The Clerk

Punctured by the quill of a prophet,
Broken by the will of the social order,
Help that sorry clerk; he needs the pity.
I tell myself a thousand times
Seek. Twist. Bend.
Lean down to lend a hand.

He is worn burlap filled with sins,
Cold smiles with evil and pins.
Appealing, appalling,
And barely strong enough
To stand alone.

I passed him by.

In his life he drank
The tea of a humble friend,
Stole his kindness,
And his gin, then sent him
On his way without his dreams.

Now that clerk himself is dead,
Covered by weeds
In a shaded grave.

Every spring I come to see him
And I don't know why.

Closed Elevator

I smell smells
You smell smells
Ha, Ha, Ha
No one tells

Cold Bed

I'll take the choice of a vision.
The woman in the grey hat sits down.
The rumbling starts
Then trembling cold
In my bed
Shivering

Cool Connie
With the funny smile
Why did you go?
Didn't you know I was going to ask
Like I did before?

What did you think
When I wasted my soul?

Communion

You and I hummed quietly
Dressed in our red and white gowns,
Facing the double doors.
As we stood, looking straight ahead,
They parted, with a familiar creaking,
And the smiling priest appeared.
We moved, graceful as angels,
Up and forward
Through the dark corridors of the great cathedral.
Eyes ahead.

It was the day of our First Holy Communion.
Two weeks after our First Holy Confession.
Seven years after our First Holy Sin.

We marched down the nave, two by two,
You and me. Hand in hand.
Sweaty, scared, and sinless.
May's warm, moist, air
Steamed us
With Latin and ritual.

A rainbow of light filtered
Through the stained glass
And the two of us looked up
To see the light as it danced
Across the open spaces,
Emerging as a flickering mosaic
Spreading a wild swirl of colors
Across the walls of the sacred chancel
As we prayed.

We thought it was pure magic,
Both wonderful and scary.
A kaleidoscope of colors
To make us smile at a time
When we were feeling the weight
Of serious thought
And too much silence.

I remember that day
When we walked
Between the bits of colored light,
With fear and pride,
From entrance to altar,
To receive our holy enlightenment.

I smile, even now, at the memory,
And long for such a straight and simple walk
To a greater peace of mind.

Concert

Flowers never sweat
And stones they never spawn.
When I finish sleeping
I'm going to mow the lawn.

My pocket knife
He has a wife
But she's not very sharp.
And when she's finished sleeping
She's going to play the harp.

The concert will be given
In the back out near the shed.
We will not wake the neighbors
Since they're already dead.

Confession

Listen Lucy,
Now that you have been purified
By your chat in the box,
I'd like you to kick off your shoes
And dance with me on the grass
Behind the church.

But first I must make my confession
To you,
And to you alone.

I confess
That I ran naked in the meadows
As you told your sins
To the man with the purple stole.

I confess
That I swam naked in the village fountain,
While you were being holy.
And I confess
That I gave a dozen old Italian women
Cheap thrills in broad daylight,
By showing them my body parts.

I confess
That I cooked these pancakes
On my Sterno
In the vestibule
Of the church
Diluting the batter
With holy water
From the fonts near the door.

I confess
That I would like to offer you
A Giant-Holy-Communion-Wholewheat-Pancake
Dotted with fresh blueberries
And dripping with butter and honey,
On this sunny day.

I confess
That I will fold it in quarters
And place it on your eager tongue,
As we swing through the sunny fields
Full of grace and dough.

Conjunctive Residues

Blue mildew on
Autumn panes,
Creeping from nowhere,
Unerasable and irrepressible,
Linking each day
To the day before.

Imperceptible advances
First vision for my morning eyes
Disregarded
Then back again
Asking for destruction,
Then quiet.

Hiding
When I am happy
Looming
When I am sad
Challenging me
To fight
Or move on.

Cote D'Azur

The sun shone with ear splitting brightness,
Baking the breast augmentations
Into leather mountains, coloring
The liposuctioned asses dark brown.
The Cote D'Azur was becoming obscene these days,
Even more obscene than it already was.

A hundred yards from the beach,
In a chapel covered with shadows,
A blind man thanked the Lord
For His kindness.

Coven

Scent of mold, muffled talk
Sacred night the maidens walk
In the forest, common trees
Hide the elk and still the breeze.

Mates the roe buck with the doe
Drops of blood from virgins flow
Stories born of women's seed
Form into a different creed.

Witchcraft cleansed of crusty moss
Is shaped into the Holy Cross.

Cyberpoems

The singing poems
Have left my home
To sit on nodes
Like cybertoads.

Croaking out
An unheard beat
On stone deaf ears
Of stone dead meat.

Daydream

Fragmentary streams of thought
Move like sunlight across
Rippled water and stop
To give me a reasonable view.

I take the reasonable view, but soon
That view escapes
Into a swirling yellow mist
And leads me down a different stream

Where cool water mixes with warm
And clear Bahama blue water
Moves upon the surface of my mind
With visions of sailboats and tanned women.

In truth, a grey sky sets the tone in upstate New York.
The blueberries of summer have all been picked and eaten
And the ice on my window sill feeds growing icicles
As I slowly drift into smooth and soothing dreams
In the gathering fog.

December and Disability

I wish I had some special girl
To share a Christmas tree
And happy loving daughters
To send some love to me.

But I have books
And pens and pills
And very little choice.
I struggle with my poetry
To find a sturdy voice.

What I have is doctor bills
And cheap whore thrills
And kidneys that don't work
And a borrowed heart
And a borrowed job
And a space down in the dirt.
Sometimes that hole
Looks good to me
For stopping
All the hurt
I think I soon will go there
In my dark blue dying shirt.

Deception

I fell to the bottom of a deep, dry well
When I was just a boy.

I hollered out to all my friends
So safe and up above,
"Will you come and save me
Just for the sake of love?"

They said they would and I was pleased
And bent my knees to pray,
"Thank you Lord for good friends' love
I witness it today."

I stopped my talk with God too soon,
As I began to tire.
Just then, my friends threw down to me
A sparkling razor wire.

Distribution of Artifacts

Part the first

The broken cage
Of an ancient hominid skull
That will go to Mr. Quill.
He needs it very much.
His wife is lonely and tense;
The skull will make her
Happy
And serene.
Mr. Quill's wife is odd,
Yet good.
She does know the way
To inner peace,
Sometimes.

Part the second

The ossified intestines
Of the extinct marsupial
Will go to Lisa,
The green-eyed girl
From anatomy class.
She was curious about
Internal parts of ancient animals.
I remember her long, slender, fingers
Running across the fibers
Of a formaldehyde soaked
Muscle.
She saw connections
Where few could.

Part the third

The small piece of broken glass,
That we removed from Tessa's foot,
With a match-sterilized pin,
One night that we were drunk,
Last summer,
That goes
To the girl
Who always sits
On the left-hand side
Of the Allente Theater
Two rows back from the front
In the third seat
From the center aisle.
She has an eye
For the precious.

Don't

Don't stand apart to condescend
When I have reached the very end.
And don't insult me with your tears
As you're repulsed by your own fears.
Don't hold yourself in better stead
Than woeful me who's almost dead.

We're all lined up in the selfsame queue;
It's just that I'm ahead of you.

Dust

Brushing off the dust
Sitting in my chair
Thinking life's unfair
Scabs within my hair
No one here to care
Slice of burning toast
Tripping on the post
Landing on my knees
Broken as the breeze

Visions in my head
Piece of burning bread
Things which I once said
Lurking in the light
A case of morning fright
Alone again at night
Thinking of the light
Thinking of
my
one
time
lover

Dutch Treat

The Dutch know how to live,
The Dutch know how to die.
When you're living in a shadow world,
It's time to say goodbye.

Duty

The angels came to her one night
But not to set her free.
They gave her special duty
To watch the night for me.

So she comforts me
And gives me tea
And listens to me cry
And when I feel like living
She makes me want to die.

Easter

Lemons grapes berries tarts
Lilacs oranges spices hearts
Grass breezes spring rain
Winter fallow field lain

Fallen angel stop near
Little child eye tear
Thought fearful mind stray
Smile fragile gone way

Home distant child think
Pause stop weed stink
Marbles sunshine girl hop
Honey butter wood chop

Trucks cars tools smiles
Knobs buttons maps dials
Sugar candy voice mild
Happy image save child

Fire in the Heart

I walked around
My bedroom
Looking for a friend.
The door was shut,
The window closed,
I started to pretend.

But I was trapped within myself
And in me trapped my heart.
The two of us look outward
But never made a start.

We could not go
We could not grow
We lived within a cage
For twenty years of silence
Until I came of age.

The door was finally opened;
I was trampled at the gate,
By loving hoards
With knives and swords
Who loved to desecrate

I ran until my fragile heart
Produced a faulty beat,
A failing heart
With fits and starts
That would not take defeat.

And so my heart
Began to burn
Refusing to be tame;
Since it would not die in prison
It set itself aflame.

Fish Eyes

Morning is seldom electric for me;
It comes like a scourge on the face.
Each ray of sun through my bedroom window
Is an acidic lash across the stone of my head.

My dull fish-eyes peer out
Blank
Unfocused
Unaware
There is a grey plastic film between me
And my world.
Most days,
I can barely see through it.

Of necessity,
There must be
A little motion
Now.

Just enough
But not so much
To make
My fish-eyes
Cry
On this sunny day.

Somehow,
I want to go somewhere;
I want to travel today.
It doesn't matter how far.
I want to talk to people I once knew,
In a place where I once felt comfortable,
In a place where things were easy,
In a place where I knew love.

Tell me toward which direction
Of the compass rose shall I turn?

Fountainhead

Sometimes,
When all is done
I feel lost
Unfathomably sad
Off-center
Like a record out of round.
There is no comic glare
No lighthearted melody
No dancing light.

Most of all
There is no music
Just the silence
Of a fountain gone dry.
Yet the dignity is pure;
The majesty is unmistakable.

This is the bed for intimacy;
The rebuilding happens now
Reintegration
From blankness and white noise

The rhythm builds and then
There is a time for turning out
New sounds
New sights
A fresh and gurgling flow.

This is the way.

Fragment

I am no poet at all;
All detractors are correct.
I write in an unsteady voice
Obscured by reason and large with timidity.
I give you unclever fragments
Dredged from parts half-know
Variously unsynthesized, raw, untranslated
Hideous and beautiful
But garbage too.

Frogs

It is that time of day when the frogs come in
Wrapped in cold wet blankets
To settle in the hollows of my mind
In the space where the forgotten trigonometry
Used to live. They linger drinking heavily,
Smoking cigars, and telling stories.
Croak, Croak.

They make me tired and unkeen
So I rest on my bed until they leave
The smoke from their cigars always lingers
And the water and slime take a long time
To evaporate.
(Poor ventilation, I suppose)

They don't do much harm
But I do wish the trigonometry
Was still there.

Fugue

Swaying branches move
His eyes, but not
His mind.
Thickets of grief
Clutter that precious
Landscape.

Harsh words streak
Like mortars in darkness
Piercing the boy's skull
With jagged shrapnel.
Fragile dreams are shredded;
His muscles twist,
Like overstretched strings,
On the edge of bursting,
Quivering dangerously
At human touch.

Back and forth
Back and forth
His hand attempts to cut
A trench through the floor,
But flesh and bone make
Useless tools.

He struggles
But the passage
Beneath his bed
Beneath the ground
Beneath his house
Is never tunneled.

In a the deep subterranean
River, the boat which waits
To whisk him to safety
Is never used.

Defensive now, he drags
The sheets around his head
And tightly to his side.
He is hermitically sealed;
It will last forever.

In a future time and place
His spinning mind replays
Memories of horror.
They come and go
Go and come
Like a fugue of despair
And terror
Starting and stopping
Fading out
Then joining hands
Crushing hope
Feeding despair
Flying in darkness
And in circles.
He is a fractured
Two-part
Rhythm of fear.

So his song spins
Day after day
After week
After month
After year.

And he is formed-
A fugitive who knows
No other song but desperation
And for whom,
The sounds of anger
Are as natural
As his interrupted dreams.

The Gardener

One fleck of rustling gray
Against a spreading field
Of orange poppies,
The gardener worked,
Silently and alone.

Rough hands
Strong heart

Straining against the memory
Of a lost lover,
Pausing to brush back the tears
Of a new beginning.

God

God is great
God is good
Like the bible
Said he should
Save the children
Cure the blind
Make me go
Out of my mind

God: Then and Now

One god
Clear voice
I pledge allegiance to thee
And me
Who are the selfsame
Thing
Divisible by two and one
And sometimes three
All at once
On a long journey
At the same time
Passing time
Eye forms
I storms.
Now
I pledge
Allegiance to me.
Free.

The Grape

I have ripened to full maturity,
In total isolation. I am
Like a single grape
On a single vine
In a large vineyard, basking
In the summer sun. Silent as a stone,
But moist. Sucking up the story
Of the dirt and sunshine.
Chronicling the flavor of the seasons
In my soul. Saying nothing, but turning
From green to blue.

Grayscale

In loneliness and darkness
Love may multiply;
With friends and ample sunshine
Love's been known die.

In the shadows
Love is forged
With blood and angry motion
Nurtured on the brittle cusp
Of darkness and devotion.

Hiding

Do you
Whisper my name
As you lie there on your comfy bed,
Eating your green
Spearmint candy?

As you squeeze
The gummy leaves
With your long, thin fingers,
And wash the sweetness down
With warm chamomile tea,
Do you
Think about the words
I spoke last night?

If I call you today
Will you pause
To hear
The subtle sound
Of need
Hiding in my voice?

Hospital Visit

There's a cold, cold, place
For tortured bones
Whose time has come.
Visit me on my way.
Alms for the poor
Gifts for the crying.

Sadden me with caring frowns;
Pity the meek.
Prayers for the frail
Are tools for the prying.

Wet a cheek and show
A tender heart.
Tears for the weak
Burden the dying.

Be sure to save
The smiles and laughs for home.
Wrinkle your brow and wring
Your hands for me.

Talk to me
About the horrors I live.
Make no jokes. Show
No lightness of heart.

Impress me with your gravity.
Save a somber mood for me;
It shows concern.

Be on your way now;
I have been your fool today.

I Believe

I believe that not only heaven exists
But that I am in it.
I believe in the pure ray of light,
First born at heaven's gate, that descended,
In pure brilliance, upon my forehead,
On a summer's night of August 1963
And showed me the way to everlasting life.

I believe in the supernatural wisdom
Of the great beyond.
And I believe in man.

I believe in the cosmic threads
That tie together all generations.
I believe in the language of the soul
That binds us all together,
Without a word.

And I believe in the religion
Of the bubbling mind,
Because it will show the way.

I believe in the crazy rhyme
Created on the night of a full moon
In a drunken stupor
As a stench rises from the bay.

I believe in the sketch drawn
In the sadness of a lonely room.
I believe in the darkness
And the evil that chases us all
To greater heights of excellence.

I believe because I am human.
And I believe that if I speak
I shall know me
And you shall know me too
And this is good.

I go away

I go away now
Like papa
No fans
No friends
No mom-bo jom-bo flowers
Piss
Piss
Stumble down
Kiss my ass

Injustice

Don't bear injustice when you see it start,
Under the guise of smiles and nods, moving easily,
Like an old familiar friend within the comfort
Of your tolerance.

Arm around the shoulder, pushing up your confidence
With that friendly touch.
Evil things can travel with grace and style.

Listen for that remark that makes you turn away,
Makes your eyes look down, glues a smile to your face
Despite your disapproval.

Your discomfort is the worm of injustice
Twisting under your skin, eating away
The parts that one time made you speak out;
They are almost all gone now.

Keeping a civil silence is habit now;
Some would call it worldliness.
Self-control is highly prized these days.

Young children have a special vision;
They see the silence hanging,
Uncomfortably, from the limbs of their parents,
Like shameful, tattered rags that would be cast off
If not for the fear of standing naked
And alone.

Interlude

A reed
A pond
A tree
Spying

A cloth
A glass
A key
Eyeing

A shirt
A blouse
A knee
Sighing

Breathing
Touching
Moaning
Crying

Tasting
Smelling
Caring
Dying.

Jazz

There are so many
Times to listen
To the music of Diana Krall
Each time with bursting
Heart beating rhythm
Igniting small sparks
On the flint of a heart
Unused.
Ringing through the pain
And the pretense,
Giving true feelings
And then more
She flutters the heart
And then...Nothing
More to say.

Jesus Beast

Sleeping, turning, churning, breathing,
Breaking through my sluggish morning mind
Each time I blink toward the window
I push out rosary beads of sweat,
Alone in this overheated room.

My holy spirit is riddled
By bullets of sun
Shot through my pink
And dusty mini-blinds.

How did I arrive in this wood-floored
Prison cell that trapped
My mind and turned my years
Into blue-green blurs of time
Streaking by like cars
Racing down the parkway after dawn?

I see myself in your baby-faced brother,
As he rushes off to class. Twenty-six
And he still gets carded at bars.
I see myself in your teenaged sister,
Making secrets and making plans,
Smoking cigarettes
As she zooms down the highway.
And mainly I see
Myself in your well-mapped
Plans

Neutralized
With hesitation.

I walked on the lawn of a wooded campus.
I was there with young boys and girls.
I played my part. My skin was smooth
My hair was black I was handsome.

Now I stand bowlegged and naked
In my New Jersey kitchenette
Squinting through the blinds
Eating cold pizza at my Monday
Morning table. Scanning traffic.
Packing lunch.

I might as well be in Nazareth,
With Jesus of Nazareth,
King of beasts and
The bad dreams.

Laura

The wind of spring
Blows cool across the city
Lovers in love
Poets in bloom
That muddy slab of a park
Is pushing up grass
Long dormant.

Laura in her light cotton shirt
Sprouts up at my place
With a smile and some daffodils
She has good intentions
But I have become cool and unyielding
Like obsidian.

A youthful heart of red hot dramas
Has been made resistant by
A middle age of private winters.
Isolation made a faithful but cruel companion
It has dulled my once eager spirit
And cocooned me in reticence and silence.

I am
Polished and smooth on the outside
I am suspended in a dilemma
I am wrapped in cool civility
I have an aging heart too fragile to reveal
One single beat of passion
Or flash of deep desire.

Until her hand rests within my tentative grip
And Laura shows me the way.

Light

Light falls from heaven
Onto my happy face
Streaming through coiling winds
Passing through fragrant pines
Through windows
Into my room
Spreading over me
Like mother's pastel quilt
Warming the musty cavern of my soul.

This lingering golden touch
Chases out my demons,
And gives me hope.
It nudges me to stir within my yellow cave;
It moves me to dress in bright colors
And share my smiling morning face
With a world
Full of lovers.

A Lightness of Mind

I feel unusually light today
As I sit here typing I feel untethered
I am floating today
At least a little bit

I go outside and
The concrete of the sidewalk feels soft
And as I make my way to the CVS
I become lighter and lighter
And am lifted completely up from the pavement

What could this be?
I haven't taken any drugs that make me drowsy
Yet I feel strange. I know I am not really floating
But it certainly feels like it.

My mind is calm and
Is not racing from thought to thought
Ideas come into my mind slowly and gently
And they linger for a while
And then they quietly move on

Then there is a long pleasant pause
Of nothingness. Today I can sense it
The ethereal space that comes between
Thoughts. I try to analyze this space
To name it. To make it tangible

And suddenly
I am back on the pavement
Clomp Clomp
My shoes are heavy
And so am I.

Lima

Lima beans, like sex machines,
Just don't have far to go.
They sit there in the pasta soup
And make a sorry show.

Then the silver shining trolley
Brings them to the dance.
Where they swirl around
Like a crazy hound
And take a little chance.

They're dancing now
I see them go
On the velvet ruby rug.
The lima in the top hat
Is hunting for a hug.

And there goes little Susie
In her costume and her mask
With the fat one who is nipping
From his little lima flask.

They had some rest,
Then all undressed,
And went into the pool.
Now, Mikey wore a condom;
He was no lima fool.

They sang and danced
And made romance
And were happy as a bean.

If I had been a lima
I would have joined the scene.

Looking

I looked at all the lovely girls
One by one
With bad intentions
Last Saturday night
At my favorite bar

Those of the soft skin
Slim waist
Ample bosom
And shapely leg

I spotted the special one
Firm and juicy
Like an orange

Gimme fruit.

Losing My Religion

What mind I had
I think I sauced it
What lunch I ate
I think I tossed it
What tooth I had
One time I flossed it
What faith I had
I know I lost it.

So here I sit —
Faithless, feckless, fearful, fool
Burned up all my engine fuel
Looking for a way back home
With a box of straw
And a long-toothed comb.

Lovers' Plans

Lovers make plans in the dark of night
Which seldom survive the morning light
Love knows no plan, or map, or chart
No self-restraint or vulgar art
Love moves like river without a start
Love moves like a river through a valley's heart

Lust

Hark, hark, the skin is soft
I 'd like to take you to my loft.
Hark, hark, my lust is ripe
Your body is my phenotype.

Dear, dear, have no fear
Bring yourself right over here
Where I can look into your blouse
And see the brick stacks of your house.

And if you catch my roving eye
Just brush my chest while passing by
And then we'll see what we can see
About a thrill or two or three.

Memories

Memories of a doggerel poem
And the time I spent alone
Writing in a little book
With a pencil in a nook

To pull from deep inside my mind
Memories that still burn unkind
Things that leave me limping left
With no warp and with no weft

Like a fabric poorly made
I begin to fray and fade
All the youngsters pass me by
I am here to speak and die.

Metamorphosis

Vines, wines, sunshine and shade
Kinfolk talking in your mind.
Precious stones shine up from the river's base
Giving birth to fresh thoughts
And dirty dreams.

Your spirit is moving on the edge
Listening to that crunchy sound
Of boots pushing down fresh
Fallen snow.

It is twisting in your mind,
The worm of a new thought
Born from a stale idea pushed
Aside by a flickering will
Strong enough to claim
More space.

Michelangelo

Cut me like a stone
With a man inside.
Chip away the extra;
You know how.

Your big hands shape
This face. The dust
In my nose is no concern
For me.

(But you should use a
Dust mask or a respirator)

Use that chisel well;
Fine features hide
Below; thin those
Heavy eyebrows,
These eyes are soft
And fine!

Smooth these rugged lips,
And please, turn the
Corners up a bit.

Big Mike,
Don't you know
I'm happy inside!

Mist

Inside her mind,
A slowly churning engine
Started to grind a fresh mash
Of anxiety and visions.

As the woman sat
At the center of a large
Public space, there was
No hiding and nothing
To comfort her
But her mind.

A schoolboy walked nervously
Across her quiet plaza;
He was alone and silent.
He had sad eyes,
And his father's cold smile.

As he moved,
People gathered,
In the corners,
Talking in hushed tones,
Through the gathering mist.

The chatter continued,
Until the boy left the space.
Then, the people raised their eyes,
Toward the woman in the center,
She remained motionless,
Silent, and calm.

Except for the churning inside.

Moments

There are times when poems flow,
With special rhythms,
And magic tones can glide
On the cool, clean blanket
Of the autumn air.

There are times when stone,
In the hands of the sculptor
Has no weight
At all.

There are times
When the dancer's movements
Tell the story
Without a single sound.

There is a summer's heat
In a winter's heart
Where a shyness of soul
Rises to break the shell
Of a frozen order.

Moonface

Moonface pulled up all of the delicate
Little trees that looked like Kanji,
As he continued to drink, heavily,
And alone,
While stomping across
A midnight blue field.

Suddenly, he reached up
To pick a piece of citrus fruit
And eat it.

Then,
He smiled-up a perfect
Semi-circle of a tangerine smile
And showed rind
Through the darkness.

Mother Earth

The plow digs in
Curling back moist ridges
Of brown vulva.

A planter follows behind
Seeding the moist folds
Pressing down fresh life

Moving on to germinate
A civilization.

The New Millennium

One
Pointed forward, toward the Apocalypse;
She gave the order to fly.
Red hair twisting in the jealous breeze,
Her beauty had no equal.
She flew, nude as Venus,
Crouched in the saddle
Of Altair.

Two
Stood tall in the stirrups
Stern and calm amidst calamity,
As they crested the Tropic of Capricorn.
Mother of them all and wisest,
Living gift of the last millennium, she
Rode unafraid through the celestial heavens
As Aldebaran surged onward.

Three
Beamed incandescent blue from piercing eyes which
Sparkled in the constellations and the cosmic dust;
She would lead the way.
Her rippled stomach was warm with sweat
And blood dripped down her back.
She was a warrior;
Antares was her mount.

Four
Spoke of poets and prophets
As she charged into the shifting winds.
Her speech was clear, and strong
Her mind most acute and
Her balance perfect.
She was the architect of the New Millennium;
Rigel carried her up with perfect dignity.

This was the shape of things to come.

New Mood

That sadness that envelops you is not the final shroud;
It is just a sleepy cloud.
If you would lift up both your arms
And swirl them swiftly with alarms

You would disperse it.

And without that misty cloud
You begin to move around
And suddenly you have found
That the state that you are in
Is not of penance or of sin
It is green grass and clear blue skies.
Drink them in with both your eyes.

Your mood has lifted.

And when you settle down
You will not find a frown
But a lightness in your soul
That is different from the old.
And all new moods are very bright
And are glittering with light.

The mood you have been looking for
Has been pounding on your door;
It's only now you've shed the fear
To open up an ear

And let the joyous sound
Come a-following you.

News at Five

When sanity was not so reasonable
When science was not so strong
When religion was a way to truth
And salvation was not a trip to the future
People knew,
Under the surface,
It all was brewing.

A dog barked as an omen.
Now the dog is sleeping
As we spin through
The cloudy skies.

Knowing how to fly
Fearing how to die
Tentative in love
Nothing is above
Spending time in queues
Eating nightly news.

Where is the girl with the golden curls?
She knew all she needed
When she was five.

Nuns

The nuns they always taught me
To waste a mind not a food.
And if you have your druthers
Be passive — Don't be rude.

The nuns they always taught me
To let myself get screwed.
The nuns they always taught me
Never to be lewd.

So when I'd grown
They had set the tone
For a living sort of hell.

But when I came to perish,
The future would be swell.

Oblivion

I am riding to oblivion
Somewhere near the Prime Meridian
Through a tube of black obsidian.
Standing upright,
Dropping fast,
Another lava core
Whizzed past.

I am naked as a jay
Accelerating
All the way.
Walls on left
Walls on right
Press me like a
Package tight
Fill my human heart
With fright
Take away my
Appetite.

I am going with a check
On a chain around my neck
To bribe the keeper of the gate
If he says that I am late.

I was human, so they'll say,
Although I never felt that way.
More a pinball hitting pins
Lots of noise but never wins.

October

In October,
I took your breath away.
You drove all day just to see me.
I was lovely,
You said.

Now,
I'm brushed aside.
Lost my blush,
Dried up,
Uninteresting,
You say.

And so I'll leave you.
But when you rest
In silent coldness
Capped in marble,
I will return.

My rosy cheeks
And October blush
Will cover your lawn
And warm your bones
With a quilt of ruby kisses.

Old Men

I know places old men go
Quiet places, unknown, nestled
In the woods, under bridges,
In the subway, in the buildings
Falling down not far away
They are places
Where no one
Finds them
Or cares to
Find them.

The One-Eyed Prostitute

Meet the one-eyed prostitute
She was cheap but not so cute.
I took her to the Bible store
Where she acted like a whore.

So I took her out to see
The Holy Manger and the tree.
Ceramic Jesus slept so sound
As the choir went around.

Then she asked me for a ride
To the place where papa lied
So I took her straight away
She was eager not to stay.

Just a moment to reflect
On the life that he had wrecked
Holy preacher man was he
Left his daughter. Age of three.

Mama was a Bible fool
Never broke a Golden Rule.
Never had a thoughtful word
Always moving with the herd.

So her daughter ran away
Losing faith and like a stray
Sold her sex to pay the rent
Meeting men with ill intent.

Bless the one eyed-prostitute
And her soul so resolute
Sturdy, willful, clever, kind
Loving, tender, wretched, blind.

Opening the Gate

When I see her
My feelings well up with such strength
I fear they will overcome me
Make me lose control
Like a hallucinating madman
Jabbering incomprehensibly on the street
Bouncing like a pinball
Between post and paddle
Yes, me, the quiet man
Sitting on the train
Right next to you.
Silent as a mushroom.
I have a great tempest inside
Chaffing to get out.

But first I must tame this tempest
And learn how to savor
My feelings in small manageable parts.
I must learn how to make my passion
Malleable so I can bend it
Shape it, direct it, curve it, soften it,
And at times, even flatten it and draw it
Into a fine gossamer thread.
All of this must come to pass
Only then can I open the floodgate
Just a crack.

Pest

I am the hole
In your brand new raincoat
I am the blotch
On your clean white page
I am the fork
In the drawer of knives
I am the sock
That doesn't match
I am the match
That doesn't light
I am the light
That doesn't work
I am the pencil
With no eraser
I am the pen
That has no ink
I am the stain
On your favorite shirt
I am the pimple on your
Smooth clean face
I am the smudge
On your favorite photo
I am the name
You can't remember
I am the crack
In your favorite cup
I am the typo
In the final copy
I am the noise
Underneath the hood
I am the wrench
That's a hair too small
I am the nick

In a perfect paint job
I am the word
You never found
I am the sugar
You forgot to add
I am the scratch
In your favorite album
I am your friend --

For life.

Pictures

At the war exhibit there were few references to love or hope
No sweet song was evoked by these scenes.
Dark canvases thick with paint twisted like pasta
Made sad fleeting thoughts ricochet around the quiet corners of my
mind
Unsettling me. Making me fearful. Like a rabbit in flight.

The industrious painter produced dozens of gray canvases
But one stood out. A rendezvous with death. A bustling
Railroad terminal exploded by a bomb. The image was dimmed
And preserved by a thin coat of shellac which saved the chilling
Horror to be seen again at another place and time.

The Poet

Onward America,
Cresting new heights of vulgarity,
Tell now of what will surely come,
The death of a nation,
Swallowed in the mire of a stagnant soul.

Sing not the songs of Amos,
They kindle no fear
Or hope.

Good friend,
Sing of me and my kind,
For we shall stir the sleeping heart
And reconstruct the City of God.
Hush now, and follow.

Possibilities

Things are know and understood
Despite ignorance;
Experience keeps an even keel
Rationing truth bit by bit.

In midnight debauchery
The glistening teeth of the young
Flash the hope of a bold generation
As they sing in their bars.

They smile,
Guided by the energy
Of their dreams
And not the desperation
Of a darker reality.

Maturity may kill them,
And they may shuck their visions
Like molted snake skins,
And try to move forward
Without a dream.

Sometimes the most promising of them
Are trampled and ignored, and
Sometimes the least promising
Will give up all hope.

Yet sometimes the sun spills down
On desperate faces and
Awakens fresh hope
For the apathetic.

Potato Soup

I can't eat potato soup
Because it sends me through a loop
Looping here and looping there
Looping in my underwear.

Looking for a place to stop
Safe from all the bombs that drop
Safe from you and safe from me
And all my pent up misery

Safe for me to take a breath
Without the thought of my own death
Safe for me to sit and smile
And craft some rhymers for a while.

But I have never found the place
That is a peaceful lodging space
So I sit here and don't eat soup
So I don't do a loop de loop.

And I pray for just one day
When the New York Times wakes up to say
That worldwide wars are gone today
And I am not going to decay

And rhyme is good for all today
Because it sends your fears away
And truth has ended all the wars
And opened up a million doors

So the people run into the street
Seeking others they can greet
And celebrate the happy day

That rhyme defeated all dull verse
And gave myself a thought perverse
That all the evil did disperse
And vanish into thin blue air
As I was combing my scant hair
And I could eat potato soup
Without the need to loop de loop.

A Prayer for Father

Death befriend him now, I hear him call you,
In darkness, from his room at end of day.
Please bring to him a peace he never knew.

In youth, kind words and gentle smiles were few,
And so a tender heart held friends at bay;
Death befriend him now, I hear him call you.

The portals of his soul now shrink his view,
Blind eyes, deaf ears, slurred speech, mark his decay;
Please bring to him a peace he never knew.

Be strong and swift and kind in what you do,
There must be no reprieve or long delay.
Death befriend him now, I hear him call you.

Thunder down in one final blinding coup
To stop the pain that breathing brings his way.
Please bring to him a peace he never knew.

Go to him now as one who comes in true,
Touch his bright blue eyes and soft locks of gray,
Death befriend him now, I hear him call you,
Please bring to him a peace he never knew.

Primate

Animus rises
In acts of subway
Madness.

Gesticulating, swerving, raging,
He bellows clearly
And alone.

He looks downward
Staring lasers
Toward steel tracks.

Savage beast
Regressed
Untamed
A primitive hominid
Receiving voices
From a distant god.

Oblivious to his surroundings
He hallucinates the divine
In a private reality.

Here is a subterranean prophet
Bold and wise.

I pause for scrutiny
I listen
I look
I learn

I am wrong.

Now
I see the hand
Pressed to the ear
Cupping black plastic
Of an ear bud.
Beep beep

This is a man
With a cell phone
Receiving voices
From a world
Far too real.

Prime

Now she pushes indignity
To the edge of injustice
With mean-spirited
Hard-hearted vituperation.

Walking on the edge of impertinence
In the shadow of insubordination
She takes umbrage
Even at the frail.

We all know
She is a prime,
So we cower
And hide.

She's not an ordinal
Or a cardinal
Chirp. Chirp.
But a prime.
Divisible by herself
And One.

And no one else.

The Primitive

Ape-man shivering by the fire
Icy moon reflected in his eyes
Hearing voices in the silent night
Looking toward the orb
Breathing smoke

Dirty hands break twigs at dawn
Working in clay under dueling moons
The voice-given visions are scraped
Onto the moist belly of his mother

Raspberry Summer

It was a raspberry summer
picking berries in the thickets with dad
First denuding one spot of berries
and moving on
Eating a few along the way
No pesticide woes
These were wild red raspberries
harvested at the expense of
so many scratches from the prickers.

I suppose no one knew we were there
in the woods near an old abandoned farm
But we liked to think someone knew
It made the picking more fun
Nothing quite as good as snitched raspberries.

I occasionally wonder if those red raspberries
are still there. Could I find them?
Would I even no where to start?
Dad would know for sure, but
he's gone now.

These days I eat store bought raspberries
when I can find them
They're so expensive
and they don't taste quite as good
as those snitched raspberries we got with dad
I remember that time in the 60's
I remember that last time, the last warm breeze
of our raspberry summer.

Ravena

Her roads make a sparse, wide-ranging scene
Abandoned cars display
Their iron-oxide-orange.

In wooden houses painted pale shades of yellow,
Generations pass through their lives
In one   solitary   space.

Not far from the high school
Quarries yield endless loads of limestone
Carved from the foothills of the Helderbergs

There are some special places where
She raises her head above the lowlands
Of a storied blue Hudson

And peers endlessly east
To the separate majesty of the Berkshires
Across the waters

I lived in such a place,
High on a hill
Where the lawn spread before me
And the lush green grass
Tried to seduce me
Never to leave.

Reason

My Reason told me one thing
And my Instinct said another
But my Instinct had no gun
So he had to run for cover.

Then Reason, like a sadist,
Pushed him down into a well
And he capped it with a theorem
So the bastard couldn't tell.

Red Dawn

Strange child in a white cotton shirt
Sitting near the willow
Glazed eyes on the rising sun.

Breezes ruffle unkempt hair
Swirling leaves crackle-up dreams.
Silent eyes
Still and slender limbs.

Quiet children, near the gate,
Gathering their courage,
Gently sweep in
Stretching arms
Fearing the loss.

His eyes never move.
The wind grows louder.

On the light
Pale Liana comes.
Fair and winsome
Speaking only to him
How he loves the sound!

The children are crying now,
Knowing his choice.
Gently she takes his hand
As they walk
Side by side
All alone.

Red Hot Chili Pepper

She was a red hot chili pepper
And she filled me with desire.
She knew she did.

It was the way she would brush
Up against me,
Leaning forward a bit
Just enough so I had an
Impure thought.

I mean she was hot.
She had beautiful breasts too
Capped with one inch tall,
Firm as fruit, red hot
Chili nipples.

In all honesty, she was so hot
That she made me a little scared
But I got over that
If you see what I'm saying.

Reservation

Two score sacks of corn meal
Lay piled inside the circle of a faded tent.
Women crush kernels on gritty stones.
Weathered faces speak,
But nothing more.

Young boys test strength
Against their fathers' bows
And each other,
Silhouettes
Against the orange curtain
Of a fading sun.
Brave warriors
In a puppet theater
Staging battles
Already lost.

Tired elders light an autumn fire;
Sensing the end most of all,
They watch the twisting blue smoke
With anger and pride
As they burn their past
And their future
Into the cold ashes
Of regret
And sorrow.

Rittenhouse Square

The canopy of lush green leaves
has thinned
but has not revealed
yellows, reds, and blues.
No doubt the show will come soon;
cold air hangs heavy
in the Square.

Highrises show
bricks through gaps,
making the Square feel small.
So much tallness all around
makes a well-shaft of
a spacious treasure.

Once robust trees show
their eerie sparseness in November,
as thin branches silhouette the seasonal
decline. Now they
look frail like my failing mother
and December's numbing coldness
seems too cruel.

Road Nap

This drunken old boy lies down
In a rainstorm
By the roadside
To catch a snooze.
The gravel looks so inviting
And the weeds by the guard rail
They don't bother me a bit.

This is my nature bed.
Cars whizzing by are music,
Beethoven's fifth, I'd say.
The insects are my friends,
Especially the fireflies
Blinking on and off.

The wet grasses around my ankles
Are my natural socks.
The rocks underneath my shoulders and neck
Are fine brocade pillows.
They prop me up to see the mist out on the harbor,
As a red sun breaks over the bay.

I'll sleep myself a perfect sleep
Amidst the gravel, mud, and rain.
And I will feel better rested when I awaken
Than you in your posture-perfect beds
With sheets
And fears.

The Rose

Men on black horses
Charged the door.
Dark blue sky made
The outer drape.
Sirius began to fall.

Three times the children screamed;
Three times defenders did not come.
One frigid breeze put
The candle out.
The children are lost
To the war.
The desecration
Is complete.

Once more,
A red-eyed child
Made a final plea,
But the soldiers would not come.

Finally, all was blood
And the scent of the rose
Was everywhere.

Sandra

Sandra sleeps silently
In the sorority of the wild rose.
Outside voices rise and fall
With smoke and passion.

Awakened,
She is sucked down
Into the loop of the dancing strangers.

She sings, sweats, smiles, and swirls
Like a shaman dancing on hot
Summer sands.
She sanctifies me,
Purging my fears
With her pulsating beauty.

Satan

I spoke with Satan the other day
And he's not so very well.
He's got a little ulcer
Because he's working hard as hell.

He's taking souls
At highway tolls
And drinking lots of gin.
His teeth are quite neglected
And he looks a little thin.

His wife is selling flowers
His son works at the grills
He wants to take vacation
But he's got to pay the bills.

Scents

Things that have no scent are flat,
Like pennies.
Boring, like starched shirts
And unlike elderberry pies
Baking in the oven which
Fill the kitchen with sweet
Smells and smiling faces.

Sweet smells are precious things.

You are a woman of smells,
Delicate, elusive, tantalizing scents.
How many of them do you have?
Are they in that little box
By your comb and brush?
I believe they are.

Before leaving for work,
I stand in the doorway
In my wrinkled shirt, watching
As you slyly put them on before I go.
Some times I smell ginger with traces of jasmine;
Other times I sense lilac and lavender
They almost always hide before I go.

Is that a lid you put on them?
Does the box keep them fresh?
I don't understand why they don't get
All mixed up in that tiny box.
I don't know how they fit.

Will you give me that smell I had last night,
The one that rippled like a blue wave?

Sestina

Thoughts of you come and go gently in my mind
Like the coming and going of a summer breeze
But summer has passed and I stand here now near the front windows
   of this old house
Looking out on a landscape whitened by the winter snow.
Branches of the birch tree droop under the weight of icicles and I
   desire
Your presence to warm the chill of this room's air

I remember that here the scent of freshly cut flowers filled the air
Today the thought of you has permeated my mind
You are reincarnated in my memory and my desires
As I open the door to go outside, a breeze
Blows out the fire I had made and the snow
Curls into a haunting drift against the silent house

There was a time when you had made a home of this now quiet
   house
And the sounds of Christmas happiness once filled the air
Now I hear nothing as I watch the spreading lawn fill up with
   snow.
Thoughts of your illness come to mind
You passed away last winter, quietly in your sleep, like the waning
   breeze
Now amount of wishing will bring life to my desires.

This heart has suffered a lifetime of shocks; therefore, I desire
This last shock to release me from its pain. This house
Is empty now and the breeze
Blows cold against the window pane. The arctic air
Is starting to freeze my mind
Numbing it so it no longer feels the sting from the coldness of the
   blowing snow.

122

I stand here to watch the swirling snow.
The happy times of my youth are all memories and lost desires.
My relatives do not seem much disturbed. They do not mind
That the spreading lawn and this white house
Will be sold by summertime and the air
That cooled our patio will then cool a new owner's house with a
    summer breeze.

Your ghost is in this house. It touches me like the breeze
And fills me with wonder as I gently touch the snow
Piling up in your summer garden. You are surely in the air
But your reincarnate form will not appear, regardless of what I
    desire.
Here, outside, I have finally composed myself and as I look at the
    house
I see your image as it lingers in my mind.

The air outside blows up a cold breeze.
My mind has settled like the snow
Yet my desire for you will linger each time I pass this old white
    house.

Shadow talk

Burgundy swirls in a glass.
Julie called for the bartender again
Smoke gets in my eyes and clothes
No excuse for a weak Cabernet
Clean the ashtray please
Mistakes can not be pinned
On me. Not this time.

Salted peanuts are
My weakness
Yum

I'll tell you
The watch she gave me
Is in the trash
Not ticking. And after
Two more drinks
I'll go home alone.
Does any body have
The time

For me?

Shimmer

A shimmer of joy in a quiet mind
Will paint the blue mood with a touch of gold,
Will reopen the door for love to find.

As a shaft of light penetrates the blind,
The sun reaches through calm eyes to unfold
A shimmer of joy in a quiet mind.

I, feeling free and strangely unconfined,
Enlivened by the sparkle of the gold,
Will reopen the door for love to find.

But tendrils with deep-rooted fears do bind
My will, while voices rise in me to scold
A shimmer of joy in a quiet mind.

Although killing the pain seems too unkind,
Cutting the roots of this familiar hold
Will reopen the door for love to find.

I act. I stand. I leave the dead behind,
To smile with my lover as I grow old.
A shimmer of joy in a quiet mind,
Will reopen the door for love to find.

Silly Putty

As a boy, I put
My silly putty
To the funny sheets.
Pulling up the blues and yellows
Pulling up the reds
Reducing my brilliant friends
To faded shadows
With every pull.

Now, in the morning
Real friends pass by
In this busy park.
We are all in our prime,
Divisible by ourselves
And no one else.

Running red-faced Linda
Sends one economical
Nod in my direction,
Nothing more to break
Her stride
Or her frustration.

Frank reads the paper as he walks.
Eyes down, a radar man,
He never looks
To see the children pass
On their way through school.

These silly-putty-mornings
Pull at me each day
Tearing at my flesh
Like a wire in the heart.

Soon my pretty Linda will
Lose the color in her cheeks,
And Frank will be my
Shadow-man-good-friend.

Simon

The father, son and holy ghost
Had lost their way one day,
And so they knelt along the road
And had themselves a pray.

Along came Simon,
On his racer bike,
And told them a good joke.
He offered them some Gummi bears,
And a fine Havana smoke.

They felt so good,
They burned some wood
And made a sacrifice.

So Simon sighed,
And then he cried,
And got back on his bike.
Paradise was lovely,
But it seemed like such a hike.

He would not trade his world
For a world so far away
He'd take a silky breeze
Across his knees
On a cool September day.

Single Scull

The wind skims my head,
Green trees and morning mist
Surround me as my oars
Cup water; I am strong
On my summer island.

There are
No crowds on the shore.
There is
No lover on the dock.
There are
No friends to help.

With each stroke
I feel more confident.
I grow more comfortable
With my aloneness,
And more connected too.

Skin Deep

I saw her in the distance
Sprawled out upon the lawn
Naked as a jay bird
Whiter than a prawn.

At first I saw her skin was smooth
And perfect as could be.
I began a conversation.
That was the end for me.

She saw that I was clumsy
And crazy as a hoot,
Fatter than a pumpkin,
And ugly as a boot.

I think she saw
My pimpled skin
And double chins in two's
A cheek that was rough textured,
Like well worn leather shoes.

I said to her, "My darlin' child,
Don't let your mind run wild.
I may not be your dreamboat
But I'm not the devil's child.

Although my skin's not pretty,
Or smooth as Gordon's Gin
It keeps the weather outside
And leaves the bones within."

Slumber

Now, I lay me down to sleep on the
Bosom incarnadine, having suffered a day
Full of indignities, I slumber now
Gently, with my head,
On your warm breasts.

Julia, you have the nicest breasts
In Christendom. And it is magical
To see their nipples stand erect
Seeking Magnetic North,
Or is it the Pole Star?

Wolf, Wolf, the bone is yours,
But the breasts are mine.

Spring Thaw

Somewhere,
In the abandoned honeycombs
Of my mind, where bright ideas
Mix with sea weed and sludge,
An image of a beautiful girl
Saves me from myself.

Skin, smiles, and eyelashes
Wisecracks and comedy.
In the morning she
Made me laugh.
In the evening she
Knew how to touch me.

With the mud of a spring thaw
And the first sound of oars
On the lake, I think
Of what we had,
And what we might have had.

Stardog

It was a curious scene by the lust machine
Where the wide-faced fool sat down.
The judo king began to sing
As the tattooed boy looked 'round.

The man streamed in
Like a violin
And the smoke whirled all around
He blew a ring
Onto the thing
The Stardog man sat down.

His mood was prickly
And his face was plain
His tone was flat as gruel.
Another ring
He chewed that thing;
The Stardog man was cool.

The people parted
And they said hello
But he didn't give a damn
He was the local prophet
Silent as the holy Lamb.

Some thought he was a lunatic
Some thought he was a fool
Some thought that he was sacred
As a vagrant holy tool.

As he turned around
He heard the sound
Of the sun come pouring in
And the people wept
As the Stardog crept
Into the street again.

Stealth Mosquito

I watched her as she approached the
Long white tarmac of Michael's arm,
As he dozed in the midday sun.
She circled two times,
Once for reconnaissance and once for business;
Landing was no casual task.

She had precious cargo.

A mine field of hairs covered the landing strip;
One accidental bump,
One errant flick of her leg,
One hint of clumsiness,
Could mean disaster.

Death was just a hair's breadth away.

But she was a stealth mosquito and
She knew how to deal
With hairy jungles.

Everything depended on it.

Instead of plowing through,
She made a hairpin turn,
Found a rare clearing,
And descended vertically.
An insect helicopter
Quick and light
And with no noise.

She turned her head downward
Toward a pink and tender spot,
And swivelled her shaft
Into proper position.

Babies need blood to survive.

She rubbed her tube briskly,
Twice from habit,
Three times for smoothness.

A smooth, clean shaft
Is the essential tool
For a stealth penetration

She paused.
She probed.
She pushed.
He never moved.

She was in.

She pushed down and drew back,
But not out.
She pumped down,
And drew back.
Down and back, down and back

Soon she would lay the eggs.

She worked,
Sucking and stroking,
Mixing saliva with blood,
Making her belly firm
And red
And warm.
When she was sated,
She withdrew her shaft and stroked it,
Twice from habit,
Three times for smoothness.
In an instant, she flew off.

She would die after laying the eggs.

A small red bump
And an itch
Would let Michael know
That she had come
And gone.

Stilton

Stilton with a little port.
I picked the scab upon my wart.
I thought about what I had read,
And then I picked it 'till it bled.

Stone Pony

After thirty-five years
I went back

My friends had gotten married
Along the way.
By and bye.
Not I.

In the woods,
The stone pony stood:
Gray, pockmarked, limestone beast,
Discolored by frequent rains,
Cracked by winter frosts,
But still standing,
Silent and dignified
After all these years.

Near the feet of the pony,
Grew the small purple violets;
They were there
When I was young.
Petals of indigo sadness,
And incorruptible innocence.

The Storm

Behind father's barn
The wind twisted straw
Around her knees.

Nearby, was the house where
Mother stayed.
Father too.
Arguing.

"Bad seed," he said,
"Bad seed."

Pale shoulders
Trembled in chill rain.
Blue lips made soundless words;
Water dripped from the faded skirt,
Encircling naked feet
With a dirty moat.

Motionless inside the
Muddy ring
Eyes down,
Bony fingers pushed against
A knotted stomach.

She knew demons,
Were casting lots
For her future.

Her head twitched,
Flooded by the acid memories
Of a broken childhood

Uncertain
That a mother's love
Would set the table
For her return.

Summer Samba

Her skin was soft and tan;
Oblique sunlight twinkled
Across the smoothing ocean
Casting a shadow
In the cove
Of her rising ileum.

All cream and coffee
Wrapped in jasmine
And transparent cotton,
The long-legged island
Girl swayed in torchlight
To the sound of a summer samba.

Innocent smile
Dark eyes
Brown torso
Gleaming lips
Bare feet
Full breasts

She
And the bosa nova beat
Made a white-hot moment
In my soul.

Sunshine

Light falls on my face
From a place far away,
She has crested the waves
And bathed the mountains;
She has traveled far
To touch me.

How I love her for it.

She dries my tears
And doubles my scent.
She washes me
In her fragile golden beauty.
She makes me handsome, strong,
And desirable
As I once was
Before the game of chance.

Susan

A raindrop slid down the driver's side windshield
To stop and spread itself out
Directly in front of my eyes
Like a tear stopping half way down
Some glassy cheek to take a rest.

It made me sad to see tears fill
The hollows of your cheeks when Susan died.
She had a hard time with words,
Always muffled or clipped.
God was cruel, you used to say.

I never thought so,
Random chance - that's all,
One convulsion of chromosomes too many,
Or too few, and sister came to us
With imperfections. So sad, but not for her.

You know she was a green-grass, beach-ball baby.
Never sorry. Never sad. Never tragic. Never mad.
All sun and laughter dancing on the lawn,
She was the happy one -
Susan with the deformed face
The defective heart
And the crippled intellect.

She gave us a lesson in humanity,
As she climbed the snow banks in the deep
Cold of a Buffalo winter to make a fort,
When she skated with us on the Turtle Pond
Behind the barn last winter.

She picked her orange-dot bitter-sweet for mama
Who placed it in a vase upon the hearth.
In her time, baby Sue was smiles and rosy cheeks
Rolling in the fresh-raked leaves of autumn
In that season just before the snow.

Sunshine girl, this tear is moving
To the bottom of my windshield,
But your smiling-sad face stays stuck
In the honeycombs of my mind
Buzzing up every now and then
When a raindrop makes me think
Odd things.

Sushi

I met her at the sushi bar
She was eating little rolls
And clumping rice
So very nice
From little porcelain bowls.

She said that she was busy
I said that so was I
But her lust for me
Was as clear to see
From the tremble in her lie.

Tea

I look for grandeur in the tea,
But the powder and shavings
Fly like glitter in the stormy winds
Of my dreams, twinkling like
Movie stars and prostitutes
On Hollywood boulevard.

I see
Down deeper
Where the tea leaves mix
With grief and fire, clinging
Remorselessly to the bottom-dwellers
Like so many barnacles on a rotting dory.

I see
Dried marmalade on the delicate handle
Splattered with the blue tears
Of a girl's melted fantasies,
Spilled from the dowry
Of her mother's pine box.

Give me a towel and lemon
So I can wash this sad cup
To the bone.

Thanatos

She comes from beyond the swaying pines
To darken these blind eyes
With a deeper shade of black.

She comes to end the pain
Of a life of empty nights,
And to fill my deaf ears
With a silence
More profound
Than I have ever heard.

Now is my moment;
She comes to take me
To the only peace
That I have ever known.

Thistles

Purple thistles covered the fields
And skin; each flower calling up
A memory.

Rock gardens can only go
So far, and looks can be
Exactly what they seem.

Memories of his tender fingers
Playing in the thick
Curls of her brown hair will dim.

Steamed artichokes and white
Wine, like the garden,
Are not enough.

A trembling finger touches
Bruised cheeks and broken dreams.
Two red gashes on her brow.

She would remember him
But not easily
Too many purple thistles

And open roads.

Thunder

The electric thunder
Astonished me
There within the smallest
Space where thoughts
Come and go
Not frightening me
Not making me cringe or cry
But awakening me to the fresh
Possibilities
After the storm

Transplant

One bleeding part
Lifted and cut
While pulsating

Quickly carried
By a sea of white and green
Sliding through long slender fingers
Drenched
By a life saving rain
Moved
To a translucent
Plastic tent
Sealed
In white
Rigid plastic.

Bumping and swaying
Through the midnight sky
Still beating
Stopping on a roof
In a dense urban smog
Rushed down corridors

The egg cracked open
The sac was removed
Still beating.
Probed, examined
Inspected for soundness

Finally stitched into
The waiting cavern of my chest
Lub dub, lub dub.

Uncle Bob

Uncle Bob
He was a slob.
His wife, she was a whore.
He drank all night
And slept all day
And passed out on the floor.

He tried one day
To change his way
His habits to amend.
But it didn't work
He had a quirk
He could not sense the end.

So he just went on dying
And no one seemed to care.
When the reaper came
To end the game
He was already there.

Vegetables

The vegetables quit their stands,
Picked up their spears, and started walking.
They joined the fighting soldiers in the front lines,
And although they did not kill, they made
A terrific distraction
For the enemy.

The cruciferous vegetables
Agreed to carry stretchers,
So the badly wounded men were hauled,
By broccoli and cauliflowers,
To a hospital five miles from the front
And three miles north
Of the River Tigris.

The vegetables talked among themselves for hours.
We allowed them their daily bread;
They gave us our daily juice.
In fact, one day we gave a sick man
A vegetable juice transfusion.
Although he struggled, he did survive,
But he sprouted a green bud from his tongue.

These modern vegetables were odd things,
Enough to make a man question his religious beliefs.
The mushrooms were the kindest of them all,
Spreading their canopies over the injured
When the rains came.

It was good for us to have vegetable support
In the war. They gave us time to act like animals,
On the road to becoming minerals,
Good food for the vegetables.

Whore

Use me like a whore
On a winter's night
And when you're done
Leave me on the bed
And go.

These white sheets
Have seen a lot of things.
I've had a lot of men
Run their eyes all over me,
And their hands too.

I've had a lot of things
Put in me,
And taken out.
I've been spread apart so many times
It's a wonder my back's not broke.
I've taken a few beatings too;
It's a difficult life,
But that's the nature
Of a good piece of
Fiction.

Winston

Winston was a swimming fish
Until I trapped him in a dish.
I sprinkled him with lime and oil
I put him in the pot to boil.
I steamed him up
I steamed him down
I sent the fragrance all around.
Soon he came out
All soft and clean,
And deader than
A jelly bean.

Wish

Wish I may,
Wish I might,
Her heart was made of anthracite.

So I struck it with my knife,
To test it for a sign of life.

A chip flew off into the skies
And sprouted wings
Before my eyes.

A pretty bird
Looked back on me
No trace of fright or enmity.

She caught the wind,
She chased the light,
She soared with unrestrained delight.

I asked if she would be my bride;
That I might travel at her side.
As I saw her turn away
She sang song that seemed to say

That she would always be with me
But she could never set me free.

Women

Some of the most intriguing ones
Live at the edge of boredom
And excitation
Simultaneously.

Moving back and forth
From node to node
From noise to silence
From listening to thinking
From moving to pausing
From loving
To something else.

They are irresistible
Whether pausing or moving
Or sleeping or talking
Or laughing or gawking
And sometimes
They are irresistible
Even when they are
Something else.

Words

I saw many words in the newspaper
And I became dizzy.
Word after word,
Word after word,
After space after word.
My mind is full of words;
My life is made of words.
Words are in my eyes,
Floating in the aqueous humor.
Words are in my ears,
Along with the wax and the hairs.
My doctor says I am suffering from
Word infection.

I must shower off the words
Even the dirty words
Along with the clean.
I must get rid of them all
In order to be free.
I must.

They attack me by air
And by see.
Words smash onto my ears,
Like rain on a tin roof,
And into my eyes,
Like bright flashes
In a peaceful darkness.

I am blinded with words;
I am deafened with words.
I need a vacation,
On an island,
With no words.

Please promise not to write.
Please promise not to send a telegram.
Please promise not to make a telephone call.

Because all the words
Are gradually making me go berserk.

I want to listen to the sound of nothing.
I want to have wordless thoughts.
Not thoughtless words.

I crave
Pure thoughts,
Pure understandings,
Unsullied by words.

These words have tortured me
Into a twisted scrap of pock-marked iron.
I can see the scars where
They scratched my skull
On the inside and the out,
Leaving it rusted orange and red.

They have forced my eyes to move
In sneaky little slits,
Narrow furtive squints,
Moving back and forth repetitively
On the page.
Who could trust a squinting fool?

I need to look up and down
And toward the corners,
As though I were trying to get an eyelash
Off my eye!
I need an eye liberation!
Therefore, I will liberate them both to look
All around and about.

And then, when my eyes travel in
Graceful all encompassing orbs,
I will hear the sound
Of the dove,
The dog,
And the crow.

Then, I will have regained my sanity
Which was driven out
By words.